Circle Needs a
Ball Gown

Lisa Rose

Printed in the United States of America
2018 First Edition
10 9 8 7 6 5 4 3 2 1

Subject Index:
Rose, Lisa

Title: Circle Needs a Ballgown

1. Geometry   2. Self-Esteem 3. Circle 4. Square   5. Rectangle
6. Triangle 7. Rhombus

Circle Needs a Ball Gown

by

Lisa Rose

The Geometry Ball was coming! All the shapes would be looking sharp. Circle wanted to look her best.

So Circle, who is big and round,
went shopping.

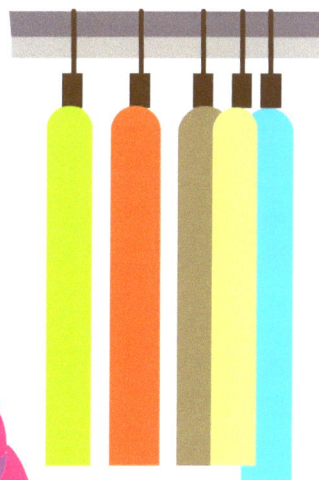

In one store Triangle was trying on an emerald green gown. Circle wanted to look like three-sided Triangle.

No matter how hard Circle stretched and pulled her curves, she could not look like Triangle whose three angles added up to a perfect 180 degrees.

Circle swirled into a different store. There she met Square who had four equal sides and four equal angles. Both of them liked the same sapphire blue gown, and they each decided to try it on.

Circle squished and squashed,
but she had to admit

that Square's angles looked all right
and her curves looked all wrong.

Circle rolled to another store where she saw
Rectangle glittering in a golden gown.

Rectangle had four right angles like Square, but only two of her sides were the same length.

Circle thought she could look like Rectangle.
So she squeezed herself tall and long, but
she still looked too round.

Slowly Circle rotated into another store and saw Rhombus shining like a diamond in her gown. Rhombus had the same length sides as Square, but two of Rhombus' angles were one size and the other two angles were another size.

Circle yanked and yanked at
the gown, but she was wide in
a different way.

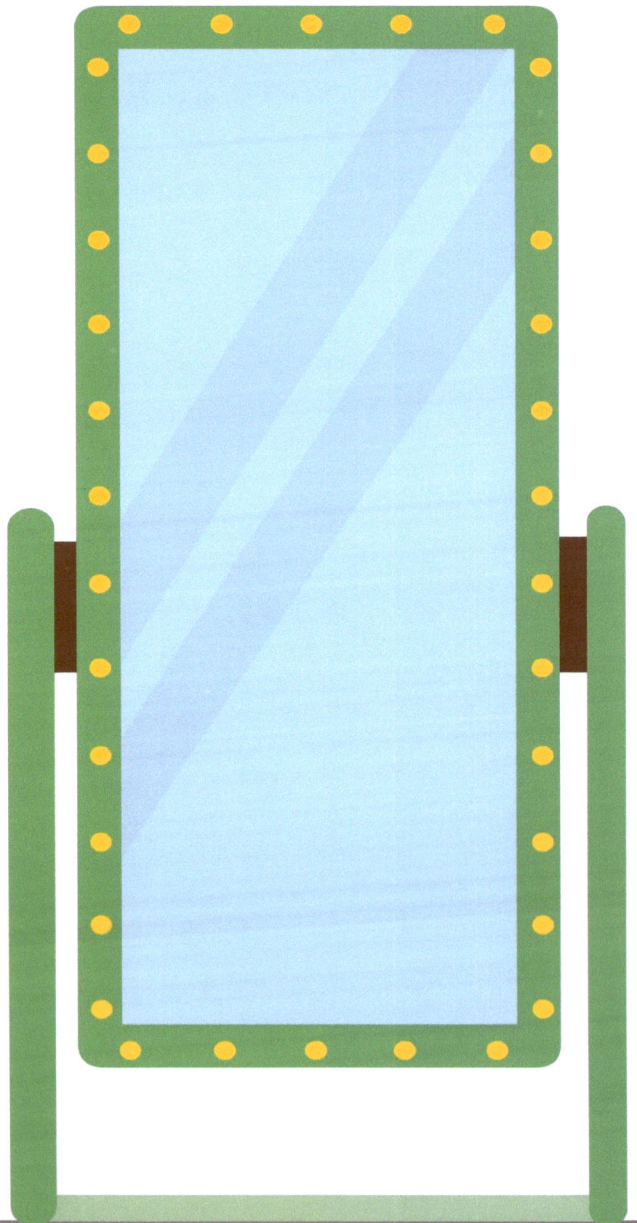

Circle rolled to the giant fountain to throw in a penny and make a wish. There she saw Pentagon prancing about in her purple gown. Circle knew what she was going to wish for. She believed her wish could come true because Pentagon had five sides. Square, Rectangle, and Rhombus only had four sides.

The extra side did not help her fit into the gown.
Circle hated her round curves more and more.

She went into the bathroom to hide.

Soon Octagon strutted into the bathroom wearing an orange gown.

Circle whirled back into the mall to find that gown. She believed that this time would be different because Octagon had eight sides and looked the most like her.

The gown did look better,
but it wasn't quite right.

Circle cried at her reflection, "Why
must I be so round and curvy?

I can't fit into anything! Now I can't go to the Geometry Ball!" A Sales Shape overheard Circle sobbing.

"Why, of course you can go to the Geometry Ball," said the Sales Shape. "We just have to find the size to fit your shape. Sizes fit shapes! Shapes do not have to fit sizes!"

Then the Sales Shape showed Circle
the most beautiful ruby red gown.

Circle spun into the dressing room.

The gown fit her round curves perfectly.

Circle twirled into the Geometry Ball.
The room sparkled with beauty.

It was the beauty of all the shapes
and sizes dancing together.

Lisa Rose lives near Detroit, Michigan. She likes to swim, eat ice cream, and practice yoga, but not at the same time. Learn more at www.LisaRoseWrites.com

www.ingramcontent.com/pod-product-compliance
Lightning Source LLC
Chambersburg PA
CBHW042106040426
42448CB00002B/162